Nostalgia

Robyn Little

BookLeaf Publishing

India | USA | UK

Nostalgia © 2023 Robyn Little

All rights reserved.

No part of this publication may be reproduced, stored in a retrieval system, or transmitted, in any form or by any means, electronic, mechanical, photocopying, recording or otherwise, without the prior written permission of the presenters.

Robyn Little asserts the moral right to be identified as author of this work.

Presentation by *BookLeaf Publishing*

Web: www.bookleafpub.com

E-mail: info@bookleafpub.com

ISBN: 9789358738582

First edition 2023

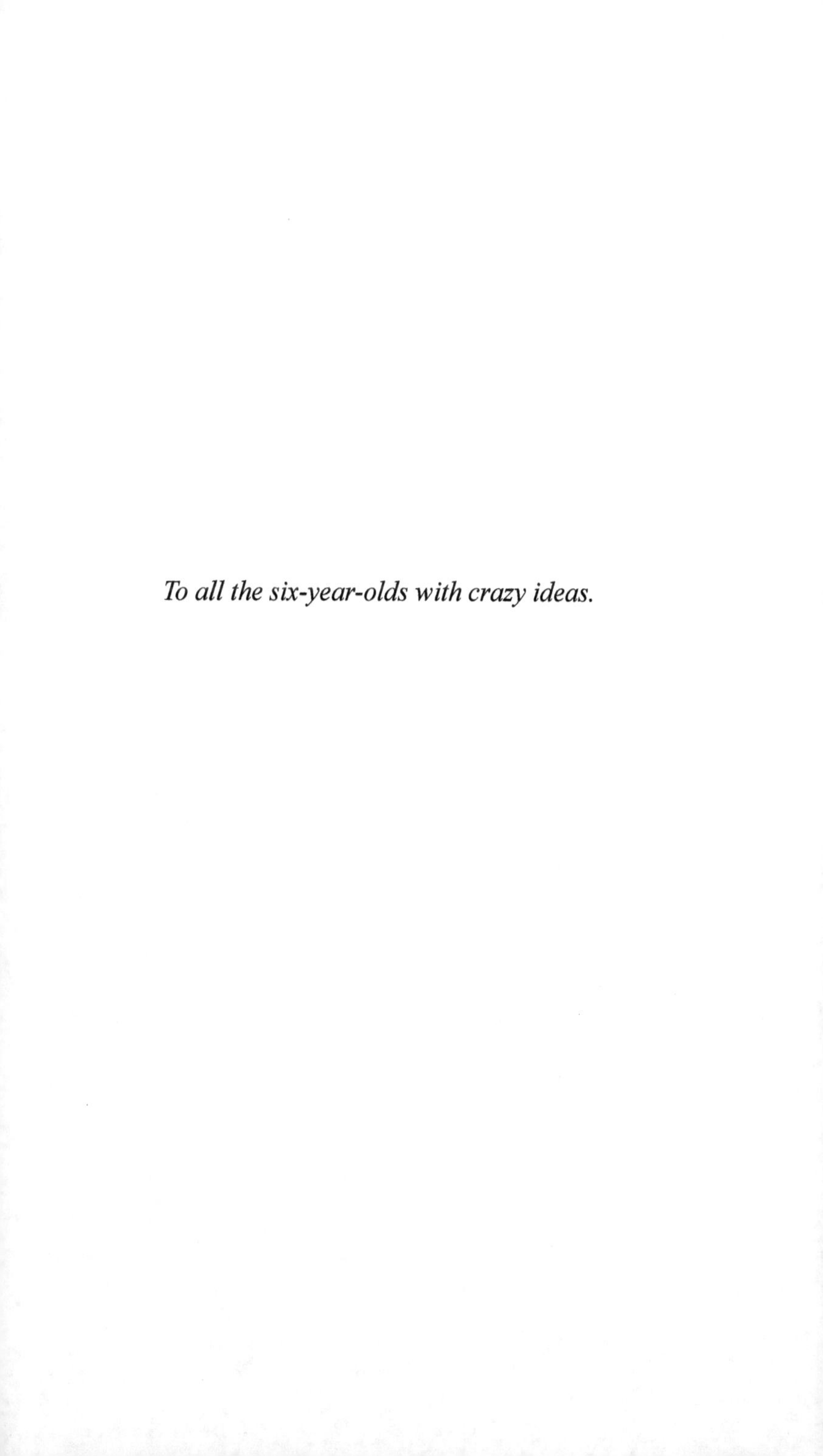

To all the six-year-olds with crazy ideas.

ACKNOWLEDGEMENT

Thanks to the people who supported me from the start and a HA! To those who did not. to the books that left me on the library floor and the many, many, used pens and knackered laptops. to the listeners from strangers on the net to my dear mother and father.

and to my grandparents whom I promised the final result.

PREFACE

nostalgia; a bittersweet yearning for the things of the past.

words on walls, the pictures forming in your head, the good and the bad, it all comes back in the end. so write it down and share it.

I Fell On My Head

My pushchair went to pieces
I fell on my head
Mum thought I might be dead
My sister kicked the remains
And me? I was a toddler with no memory
The anger and tears came from them, not from
me
My skull is cement and I still live
It doesn't show does it?

Child Pride

The wall was littered with messages
Seniors had written their names
So the playground would be haunted
With their memories
I would drag kids to point out a certain name
"That's my sister!" I would exclaim proudly

Moving Around My Room

I never sleep without the street light
Curtain ajar, the crack between
The bed and the window visible
So I can see the spiders coming
So the shadows in the wardrobe
Don't move every time I blink and
Whatever is under the bed is the
One trapped and not the child
Still dreaming wide awake.

Joshy

When I was five
I wanted a cat, not a dog or even a tiger
The animal that I favor
Things that would later come to pass
Two goldfishes to ease the gap
Then I met the neighbor's cat
A young tabby man named Joshy
Wanting the love he didn't get during the
daylight
climbing into the house and on my head in the
night
Until his owner came home to him

Maps

Golden Gate is a bridge to the other side
Eiffel must be a ladder to the sky
Is that Uluru?
Or is it a shaggy dog resting

Outstretched she looks up
There is a wall of islands
she rests her head against
feet dangling over the edge
And the floor is death
Should she dare
to plunge below

Memories plaster a rectangle world
A square of roots planted down
Of foreign corners roamed around
Mementos of other lives well-lived
So very unlike her own.

And yet her world expands
An eagle soars in her head
Color below apricot and green
Above blue, black, and grey
Now she dreams atop cliffs
Towers above stretching on end

Giant and so beings of shapes
That shrink as she grows closer
Closer than those before her

No bitter taste reaches her yet, she's far too
young.

Places she'll never see again
That one day will be faint in her head
She'll still hear and smell and feel
Experiences clear to her eyes
As the days occur
And then dry out moments later

No, This innocence can't die
Not just yet
Maps are lives lived well
And this little girl should
draw her own map
The size of the world

Poverty

We're not poor, not really

I know we aren't rich
I once saw a man-coated
Filth, feet bitter with cold
Yet the streets of London
Passed him by
We're not poor like that

I saw people packing up their lives
To live on the streets or a friend's spare bed
I've met people moving from place to place
Just trying to find a friendly roof
We're not poor like that

But the dust on your floor
Thickens every hour
A pound in your pocket
For the bus fare
You vow to follow goals
In the same shoes
yet cheques can bounce
And You go under
At the drop of a hat

Do you plan to live off your folks
They ask tone snide
Like outside the front door
The answer is waiting after a knock
I'll take matters into my own hands
Before I stand in the endless queue

But who passes the first test?
Some evade before birth
The ugly truth of such heights
Nature vs nurture
Greed or charity
You already know
A few dollars more
And they'll loathe you

A friend once said that
If someone had more than £100
She'd wish them instant death
I'm not going to eat the rich
I just want to be better than them

Finicky

What is it that you can eat?
I can't eat chicken, I can't eat bologna.
The bacon was kind of dry
So what if I miss breakfast once or twice?
I don't like eggs. I don't like beans.
I won't touch carrots or cheese.
At mealtimes, I might eat to humor my parents
At gatherings, I might eat to humor my friends
But once they are all gone it will come up again
They can ponder why all-day
Soon they promise your tastebuds will change
But for now, my food still can't touch on the
plate
I can change. I have all the time in the world.
Maybe I'll start tomorrow

I'm not obese. I'm not that skinny.
I'm just picky.
Everything's fine.
I'm fine.
I'm fine.

Pimples

Pimples! Pimples! Pimples!
Coming day and night, blind and ingrown
Pustules on my nose, cysts on my forehead,
All over my jawline, down my back, and even
my rear end!

Every day I wash my face
Then I rub in some cream
Add on more tidbits before
I allow myself to be seen

Can a scarf cover it? It'll have to do!
I can't go out in the sun while the cysts remain!
God forbid everyone knows I picked like a fool!

What's that?! A blackhead on my face?!
Any more and I'll scrape it all off!
A drop of cider vinegar a day to keep the
redness at bay

I think my face is clear! Now there is nothing to
fear!
Everyone knows as you age the scars will fade!
I hope it is true and God has forgiven my sins
But I have to wonder what was that on my
grandma's chin

Lazy Saturdays

Summer mornings in a spare bed
entertainment available by 7
breakfast and then back at 11
curtains ajar to spy a crack of light
I'll close away the rest of the day
and the next thing you know
it's dark outside and you're alone
where did all that time go?

I Broke My Bed

12

It's the facts of life
You're having a good day
When your mattress breaks
The springs burst through and cut you
You're sleeping hard rather than saying a word
They sandwiched cardboard halfway
It's bent and you have to find a new place to
sleep anyway

Crowding an Empty Room

First, it is bare
Then the books come in
Scattered on the floor
Add a few toys as well

You'll need a Chair and desk
Maybe a bed
Or a sofa doubling as a bed
A fridge would be brilliant
Or at least a working toaster

I could set up entertainment
From the roof to the floor
Shelving photo and video
And still room for my game console

Maybe I can get creative
One side a study the other a dancehall
Maybe a pool and a bowling alley
Knock a hole in the wall for an alcove
Or even a pizza oven!
Turn the lights off and it's a home theatre
What were we talking about again?
Oh right, crowding an empty space
Just put the boxes there for now
It'll still be there later

The Last I Loved The Cold

I still came up to your knee
Five and feeling my wellies crunch
Two years and the fields are white
Running in the snow until the bite sets in
Eight and nine my fingers are red
Ten I slip over on the ice and hit my head
Twelve and I get a snowball to the eye
Three years each snowed in
And warmth becomes a pleasant surprise
That's the last time I loved the cold

The Short Walk

15

The short walk is less than a mile
Rocky, close and perfect to be punctual
The long walk is a mile but a sight
For the sore eye

Dying in bed...ok it's a cold

My face is warm
My body is humid
Yet part of me is still so very, very cold.
How long have I been here?
All I desire is to disappear
And finally
I rise
Forgotten by my eardrums, ingrained into
memory, All day and all night
I received an ant bite dead center of my belly
one year
Having a friend, That's the best medicine

I Went Down Into The Woods Today

Summertime, wellies, and raincoats on
Papa had his cap and walking stick out
Into the woods, we go
Over autumn leaves and wooden gates
Into the woods, we go
Walking across trees and slippery banks
World of creatures
Stripey horses. Giant kitties, swamp monsters
The world is full of strange beasts
You'd never believe me
Once they said there was no such thing

Picture Book House

Figurines on the mantelpiece
Wooden animals and china women
Tell the tale of dramatic romance or enchanting
hybrid stories

Suddenly I hear chiming music
Silver and gold instruments lining the cabinets
sway with tunes
The Paintings come to life
Day and night they move
Along a river in Africa at sunset Or a marsh in
the European coasts

No noise but a ticking clock in the night
The soft carpet is both sand and grass
While the garden is a jungle
And every passing cat is a tiger
The rockery is a pond, a river
where wild salmon are hunted
By a bear jaw slung on a hook
feathers strewn along the ground
Once belonging to the trees
bones that you try to not step upon

When you turn to look back

The house appears still life
Picture an attic a story above
A secret above a trapdoor
Creating childish mystery
The spooks lie in the woods
The walk is already daunting
The houses in front crooked
They jumble like a labyrinth
You walk the other way

In your mind's eye
The roof is coral blue
The flowers paint tales
The door moves on its own
Then laughter fills the air
Down the path away from
This little picture book house
Images follow as you descend
Off the walls comes the highwayman,
A bird's caw, a lady with a beautiful voice
Along the picturesque street, they follow
Down the uphill, you may find a cat wandering
it's own tale down the alley

Can Never Say Goodbye Right

How long do I have until I leave?
I have slowed my pace, You are ahead of me
Have I said what I want to say
I haven't said what I needed to say
cruelest of all it was a bright day.
You are already ahead of me
The unease in my stomach
The tension in my fingers
I know deep down
What we promise will never happen
I can't forget
I won't forget
Sorry but I can never say goodbye right

My New Favourite Holiday

Only one time do we gather round the table
After receiving socks full of gifts and
Allowed to see what was meant for kids

There are lights of many colors
One for each celebration
Pastels for the day of the sweets
Gothics for the night of the creeps

In the middle of the night, you can
Be whoever you want and you
Don't necessarily have to fear
What you can't see

Or when the sun is out
And you have weeks of freedom
Stretching ahead and no one
To stop you if you
Can't get out of bed

Holidays are there for you
Can you make one for you?
My holiday is a weekend
Certain songs, certain books,
And I celebrate it once a month
So Yes, you can make one up

Hiding in the Hallways

Down here no one can see me
Sure the halls aren't empty
I'm thinking of going out
But I'd have to dodge people
Nobody cares about the corner
So I can hide in it
Working things out as I go
Turns out the closet is too small
But nobody notices in a busy hall

Stutter

I never had a stutter
Growing up I'd almost never speak
Or my voice would never stop
So maybe on occasion
I stumble when I speak
But I become clearer
And I break the silence

That would be the perfect end
Except it gets harder to talk
With harsh eyes and stunned brains
Focusing becomes more and more
Like trying to speak with eyes
And soon, thinking is better than
Clarity and it takes a while to
Start back up again
Now I'm an adult with a stutter
Trying to learn what to say again.

Resurface

Just leave me here and I'll come out in 300 years
She said, she said, hiding behind the blue door
But it's all coming back now
The forgotten first friend. That forgotten first
school run
The first suffering, the first goodbye,
With all the bad you remember the little things
That made it through for you

You learned to read, you found the places to go
in need
And it's over, you just remember.
It resurfaces but it will go back down soon
And you took a look
The blue door has been painted red

www.ingramcontent.com/pod-product-compliance
Lightning Source LLC
LaVergne TN
LVHW021342200726
843509LV00014B/2630